A GIFT FOR

⁂ FROM ⁂

THE
PUTTER'S
POCKET
COMPANION

THE
PUTTER'S
POCKET
COMPANION

JIM MCLEAN and
DR. FRAN PIROZZOLO

BOOKS

HarperCollins*Publishers*

BOK 5004

Published under license from HarperCollins Publishers, Inc.

DESIGNED BY JOEL AVIROM & JASON SNYDER

The Library of Congress has cataloged the original edition of this title as follows:

McLean, Jim.
        The putter's pocket companion / Jim McLean and Fran Pirozzolo. —
1st ed.
            p.   cm.
        ISBN 0-06-017189-8
        1. Putting (Golf) I. Pirozzolo, Francis J. II. Title.
GV979.P8M35   1994
796.352'35—dc20   94-18734

ISBN 0-06-095461-2 (Hallmark edition)

99 00 01 02 03 RRD 10 9 8 7 6 5 4 3 2

FOREWORD

Good putting skills allow low-handicap golfers to score birdie when they hit a green in regulation, and medium and high handicappers to save par when they miss one and chip the ball several feet from the hole. Hence the old adage, *Drive for show, putt for dough.*

The putting stroke is the simplest-looking technique in golf, involving the least degree of muscular strength and coordination. Yet it's the one stroke that's the hardest to perfect. In fact, many golfers find it easier to whack a ball 250 yards straight down the middle of the fairway than to sink a 2-foot pressure putt. Putting, therefore, is without question the most frustrating department of the game.

The last time I putted exceptionally well was in 1976, at the Crab Meadow Golf Course, a relatively long layout located in East Northport, New York, near Long Island Sound. I shot a course record 68 that day.

The reason for my success was a putting key that I discovered on the practice green before the round. It involved raising my hands higher at address and thinking of the back of my left hand as a secondary clubface. "Just keep the back of your left hand square to the hole, and the clubface will point straight at it," said a voice.

Since that day I've tried that very same tip at least one hundred times. It never worked again. You know the reason. If you've played golf for any length of time, you've probably learned the hard way that you can't depend or survive on *one* tip alone.

Even the best putters in the world depend on a different key every day they play—or at least they try to. One day they'll think *low and slow,* meaning they'll swing the putter back low to the ground and at a smooth tempo. Another day they'll think of keeping their head *perfectly still* because that will protect their body from swaying and thus prevent a mishit. The trouble is, some days you can't remember an old tip. On other days, no new tip comes to mind.

Why golfers experience such difficulty on the greens has remained a mystery since the game began in Scotland around four hundred years ago. Not any more! Jim McLean, one of golf's top instructors to the pros, and Dr. Fran Pirozzolo, the renowned sports adviser who is a mentor to the game's premier players, have studied the great putters of the past and present. In the process, they have discovered why golfers miss. But more important: they have devised *one hundred* unique keys for putting well, and they have put them into *The Putter's Pocket Companion.*

McLean, who works with many PGA and LPGA stars, will provide you with top tips on the physical side of putting. Pirozzolo, who teaches the best putters in the world, offers an equal number of tips on the mental aspects of putting.

McLean is essentially a fundamentalist who focuses mainly on the basics. However, his tips are anything but evergreen— they are innovative. For example, he suggests looking at the hole while you stroke a putt if you're in a slump, and going southpaw style if you suffer from the putting twitches, or *yips.*

Pirozzolo's tips revolve around imagery and commitment to practice and offer immediate on-course remedies for common putting problems.

Just reading the introductory dialogue between these two wizards in the world of golf truly convinced me that I could putt well again. I was excited because I finally wasn't hearing the same old fluff but rather new instruction on putting that is based on years of analytical research.

I'm off to try one of McLean's physical tips right now. If it doesn't work, I'll try one of Pirozzolo's mental keys for improving my putting. Chances are one tip will work today—so I'll save another for tomorrow.

—John Andrisani
Instruction editor, *Golf* magazine

INTRODUCTION

PIROZZOLO: Jim, it's often been said that great putters are born not made. As the man who spent huge amounts of time with one of golf's top putters, Brad Faxon, answer this question for me: can you teach golfers to improve their putting significantly?

McLEAN: Yes, I think every golfer has a chance to become a much better putter—to become a master of golf's *ground* game—if he or she pays closer attention to certain fundamentals.

PIROZZOLO: So it's only a matter of focusing on some technical fundamentals or basics.

McLEAN: No. I feel that the physical side of putting is important. I also know that the mental side of putting is an essential link to good putting. And, of course, we both know how vitally important practice and knowing how to prepare yourself are to putting well consistently. Therefore, in *The Putter's Pocket Companion* we'll include tips not only on stroke, stance, alignment, choosing a putter, and reading greens but also on the important mental side and, just as vital, on how to practice—how to learn to get better—and on how to gain confidence in your mechanics and in yourself.

PIROZZOLO: Great, Jim! I'm ready for the challenge. Let's get started with those fundamentals you were talking about.

McLEAN: In the most basic form, most great putters set their eyes either over the ball or slightly inside the target line. They also position their arms and hands directly beneath their shoulders, point the toes of both feet directly at the target line, assume a light grip pressure, and use a simple stroke—one in which the putterblade remains low to the ground and square to the target line on the backstroke and downstroke. They use one arm or the other to pilot the stroking action.

PIROZZOLO: Beyond the setup and stroke elements, have you discovered that there are other similarities?

McLEAN: Yes. Based on many years of studying the strokes of past and present-day putting masters, I've discovered that all great putters also:

- ▶ Follow a set prestroke routine;
- ▶ Read the break in greens expertly;
- ▶ Know that the slower a ball moves, the more break affects it;
- ▶ Know that speed control is the key to judging the break and eliminating three putts;
- ▶ Focus their attention on the target before triggering the stroke;
- ▶ Relax their shoulders, arms, and hands;
- ▶ See the ball rolling along a particular line and dropping into the hole before they putt;
- ▶ Hit the sweet spot of the putterface time after time;
- ▶ Contact the equator of the ball.

PIROZZOLO: That answers many questions about the basic fundamentals. Who are some of the all-time best putters who have used or use fundamentally orthodox styles?

McLEAN: Ben Hogan, who putted great during his heyday in the 1940s and 1950s, was very orthodox. So were Jackie Burke and Sam Snead. Bob Charles, George Archer, Greg Norman, and Nick Faldo—all excellent putters—also fall into this category.

PIROZZOLO: Who are some of the all-time best unorthodox-style putters?

McLEAN: The late Bobby Locke, the great South African player, set up closed—aiming feet and body well right of target—and felt like he hooked the ball into the hole.

Isao Aoki, from Japan, sets the putterhead in a very exaggerated toe-up position, picks the putter well off the ground on the backswing, then chops down on the ball.

Gary Player still uses a hit-and-hold punching style, or *rap* stroke.

Arnold Palmer still sets up pigeon-toed, but not quite so much as he did when he ruled the links. Like in the old days, he also uses an extra-wristy stroke.

Billy Casper has always used a wristy pop-stroke, similar to that employed by Bob Rosburg, another absolutely spectacular putter.

PIROZZOLO: How can a player be successful consistently using a very unorthodox putting technique?

McLEAN: Fran, you can answer that question just as well as I can—you've watched your friend Bernhard Langer go from the world's worst putter to the world's best putter. How did he do that?

PIROZZOLO: I can't take credit for what Bernie accomplished to turn his putting game completely around. As you know, he invented a personalized cross-handed putting grip, and he's experimented with a putter or two, including one he purchased from a pro shop barrel at Sunningdale Golf Club, in England. I can, however, tell you something about the mental skills he used to overcome the yips.

McLEAN: I've heard so much about the yips and I've heard many different explanations for them. You're a neuropsychologist, I should ask you.

PIROZZOLO: The yips are sometimes called *focal occupational dystonias*. They are involuntary movements: jerks, twitches, and freezing, usually in the hand and arm. Some studies say one in four golfers have experienced the yips. They're more prevalent, of course, during tournament play when the pressure is more intense.

McLEAN: Didn't Henry Longhurst, the world-renowned golf commentator from England, say about the yips, "Once you get 'em, you never get rid of 'em?"

PIROZZOLO: Yes, he did, and most golfers fear the yips because they think they'll never go away.

McLEAN: Then how did Langer rid himself of the dreaded yips?

PIROZZOLO: Two ways: diligent, intelligent practice and incredible self-trust, or confidence. Nobody works harder and nobody believes in himself more than Bernie.

I think confidence is a major reason why a player can overcome the yips and the main reason a golfer can putt well using an unorthodox style.

McLEAN: How does a player become a more confident putter? Sometimes I've noticed it can be a matter of buying a new putter that feels good and is aesthetically pleasing to the eye. Do you think that's enough to turn things around, just to give a player a fresh outlook?

PIROZZOLO: Yes, but those fixes usually run their course in a short time.

McLEAN: What do you think is the ideal way to develop long-term confidence? Let's face it, putting is a big part of the game; you'll never score well unless you putt well.

PIROZZOLO: That's right for sure. You'll never become really confident until you putt well. And, ordinarily, we think that to putt well we have to practice a lot.

McLEAN: If that's the case, then why aren't all the pros on Tour great putters?

PIROZZOLO: Because most professionals only practice the stroke. They don't practice *smart,* and they don't practice mentally. I might ask you why amateurs don't putt well.

McLEAN: They rarely practice at all. If they do, they tend to think that making a few three-footers is practice. I enjoy taking motivated students out on the course and inventing practice routines, games, and challenges.

PIROZZOLO: Jim, you've helped me and other amateurs, and professionals too, through drills. As you know, I'm constantly amazed at how poorly golfers prepare. My studies with the National Academy of Sciences Committee on Techniques to Enhance Human Performance affirmed this conviction. We golfers are the worst at practicing, at preparing ourselves to compete.

McLEAN: What are some of the principles you'd suggest for some good practice habits?

PIROZZOLO: For starters, a good rule of thumb is that sessions should include 70 percent physical practice and 30 percent mental practice. We've both seen our friend Lauri Merten, who won the 1993 U.S. Open at Crooked Stick, improve her practice. This had a direct positive effect on her putting performances. In fact, in 1993, she was second on the LPGA Tour in putting. To what do *you* attribute that kind of improvement?

McLEAN: Lauri works hard and she works intelligently. I've seen her here at Doral working constantly on putting drills designed by Mike McGetrick, her teacher when Mike worked at my Learning Center. Dedication, discipline, belief in her system and herself are other reasons why she has succeeded.

PIROZZOLO: That's right, Jim! Because putting is both physical and mental, there are so many ways you can help a golfer to improve. Improvement takes the help of a good coach with a great imagination.

McLEAN: What practice methods do you recommend golfers use to improve their putting skills and confidence?

PIROZZOLO: In practicing the mental side of the game, golfers can learn from athletes in other sports who are totally committed to visualization before they compete. Football players, for example, do brain warmups before taking the field. Wide receivers sit in the locker room with their eyes shut, rehearsing pass patterns in their heads. They continue meditating until they see themselves being bumped by a cornerback, then running down the field making a head fake toward the safety, then making a sharp cut toward the sideline. Ball, both feet in bounds. Roar of the crowd. Fade to black.

This kind of mental practice by athletes—a visualization primer of the proper moves necessary to perform a physical act—has been going on since ancient times.

Golfers who want to improve their putting should ideally spend fifteen minutes a day visualizing their prestroke routines and actual strokes.

McLEAN: What about concentration? Can that be intensified so that the visualization process is more vivid?

PIROZZOLO: Absolutely. It's no surprise that the golfers who can focus best win the major championships. Bernhard Langer, Jack Nicklaus, and Greg Norman are the best in my book.

McLEAN: What's their secret?

PIROZZOLO: They recall past successes, focus their minds on what to do (never on what not to do), visualize the perfect execution of the stroke, see the ball drop into the hole. These mental rehearsals clear your head, thereby preventing distraction, anxiety, and overtrying.

As an aside to the great concentration of the pros, let me comment on another athlete. Jim, you've helped NFL player Al Del Greco to become a better golfer. As his caddy in several major events, I have tried to make sure he keeps those McLean images fresh in his mind so that he knows what he wants to do, instead of getting distracted by what he doesn't want to do. He's been quoted in scores of interviews recently, claiming that his success in football is caused in part by what he learned in golf. The reason is that those positive thoughts clear his head of anxiety.

McLEAN: What other ways are there to reduce anxiety?

PIROZZOLO: The simplest way is to relax any excessive tension that usually builds up in our hands, arms, shoulders, and face. A deep breath or two a few seconds before you stroke a putt will work wonders, too.

McLEAN: These days we hear a lot about how mental toughness is what separates good athletes from great athletes. How important is this element to good putting?

PIROZZOLO: First, Jim, I agree unequivocally with what you've heard. Mental toughness is the most important skill you can ever have. It is not an innate skill, rather it is learned through practice. Second, mental toughness should not be confused with a macho, win-at-all-costs, in-your-face attitude. Lauri Merten exhibited all the mental toughness you could ever want in birdieing the last three holes of the 1993 U.S. Open—all with a smile on her face!

Mental toughness on the greens is having the poise to stick to your routine—not to be overcome by the pressure. It involves visualizing past putts you holed under pressure; being physically relaxed but mentally aggressive; going for the hole and knowing that if you knock the ball past it, you'll make the come-back putt; having the ability to control your thoughts and emotions when a putt hangs on the lip, or when you sink a very long putt; having the ability to find a positive way to respond to missing a short putt.

Another element of mental toughness is the ability to shut out all negative thoughts and replace them with positive self-talk. For example, say you're standing over a three-foot putt to keep the match even and force it into extra holes or sudden death. Instead of thinking about the pressure of the situation, tell yourself this: "Okay, it's crunch time. This is why I love golf so much. I'm having fun. I will love holing this putt." It's this kind of positive, goal-directed, focused arousal that prevents you from choking.

McLEAN: Is it mental toughness that allows a golfer to stick to and repeat the same prestroke routine every time he or she putts?

PIROZZOLO: Yes, and I'm glad you brought up the routine. An often overlooked cause of poor putting is a prestroke routine that is inconsistent or flawed by inclusion of irrelevant steps and details, or omission of important steps and details. The prestroke routine is based on the assumption that we must gather information about the environment (for example, length of putt, slope, break, etc.) and program this information so that our internal coordinates can be matched to the task of making the putt.

The number-one problem that most players have in their prestroke mechanics is poor target orientation—in particular, they spend a great deal of time reading a break in a green and do not allow their natural athletic brain to gauge the distance and, therefore, the length of stroke. If you can achieve a quiet mind your brain will naturally compute the correct length of stroke, and this will happen as naturally as it does when we throw a ball to a target. We do not have to provide our brains with unnecessary verbal information during the ball-throwing task— we don't say we are twenty-eight feet, six inches from a target with a fifteen-mile-per-hour wind quartering left to right. We rely on our brains to make these calculations effortlessly.

Rely on your natural athletic gifts to respond to the target. Focus your attention more on the target than the ball. The ball isn't going anywhere. Once you have trained yourself to stick to your mechanics, your stroke will also be on automatic—so that now you will be able to attend to the relevant stimuli—the target.

McLEAN: You have covered some great points on the mental side. What's involved in practicing the physical stroke?

PIROZZOLO: In addition, Jim, to practicing stroke mechanics, golfers should play putting games under different kinds of conditions. It's extremely detrimental to practice the same putts on the same green all of the time. Here are three putting games that will help any golfer improve.

1. Putt from a long distance, say forty to fifty feet. If you miss the hole, move the ball back one putter length, so that you never have a tap-in. Try to two putt as many times as possible.

2. Take an eight iron or nine iron and chip from a fairly easy lie forty-five to sixty feet from the pin. Try to make five consecutive up-and-downs in two strokes.

3. Try to make five to ten consecutive two putts from twenty to thirty feet with your eyes closed. This will develop feel, muscle memory, or what I call *internal representation of the stroke.*

Jim, you've got some great advice on practice. Let's hear about your views.

McLEAN: I think that first and foremost a student should often simulate the game condition by practicing putting with just one ball. Instead, I'll see amateurs practicing with several. In a short time they become bored and they start experimenting with silly setup positions and strokes.

Practicing with one ball before a round of golf readies you for the course situation.

PIROZZOLO: Are you against experimentation?

McLEAN: Not at all. In fact, I'll go so far as to say that if a player has tried tip after tip and still can't putt, he or she should turn around and putt the other way, i.e., a right-handed golfer should putt left-handed. If that doesn't work, try what Johnny Miller did one year when he won at Pebble Beach. He putted while never taking his eyes off the hole. Experimentation is a good thing if your putting is miserable. There's no point in experimenting before a round if your normal setup and stroke work.

PIROZZOLO: Any other commandments of putting before we begin our one-hundred-tip putting lesson?

McLEAN: Yes. Relish the moment when it's your turn to putt. Act! Let the green be your stage. Take charge and enjoy the experience, the challenge! Look confident and professional.

You can usually tell just by watching his or her body language whether or not a golfer knows what he or she is doing and, further, whether the golfer will miss or make a particular putt.

THE
PUTTER'S
POCKET
COMPANION

If you've had a bad season of putting, try an old putter from your collection in the garage or buy a new one (after you've tested it out on the practice green). Often a fresh start and clear head are enough to get you going again.

*Trying a new putter can sometimes help
you recover from a putting slump.*

ACCELERATE THE PUTTER

One of the basic elements of good putting is to accelerate the putter in the impact zone, while keeping its face square to the hole. To promote the proper action in the hitting area, keep the handle of the putter moving *toward the target*.

Most good putters let the putter's handle play the "lead" on the downswing.

WHEN IN DOUBT, PLUMB BOB

No matter how well you read greens, occasionally one will baffle you. In these circumstances, *plumb bob* à la Ben Crenshaw to figure the break. Here's how:

Hold the putter in front of you, with your right hand grasping the grip (lefties reverse instructions). Obscure the ball with the lower part of the putter's shaft before looking straight ahead with your dominant eye (close your other eye).

If the shaft appears to the left of the hole, the ball will break from left to right. If the shaft appears to the right of the hole, the ball will curve to the left.

Depend on the plumb-bob method when confused about the break in a green.

WHAT TO DO ON SLOW PUTTING SURFACES

On slow grass greens, play the ball farther back in your stance and put 60 percent of your weight on your left foot. This type of setup decreases the effective loft of the putter, because it encourages your hands to be positioned ahead of the ball. It also promotes a slightly downward hit that's best on slow surfaces.

When putting on slow greens, play the ball farther back in your stance.

WHAT TO DO ON FAST PUTTING SURFACES

On superfast greens, use a *heavier* putter, which is much easier to move slowly than a light putter. Be sure, too, to employ a smooth, even-paced putting stroke.

A heavier putter works best on courses featuring very fast greens.

HOW TO HANDLE BIG LEFT–TO–RIGHT BREAKERS

Play the ball off your left instep in an open stance to ensure that the putterface hits the ball as it's almost closing. This strategy is good because it virtually guarantees that you keep the ball on the *high* side of the hole.

Play the ball forward in an open stance when facing a left-to-right putt.

MINIMIZE YOUR WRIST ACTION FOR SUPER CONTROL

If your direction and distance control are both off, chances are your stroke is too wristy. To assume a very secure grip and take the wrists out of your stroke, drape your left forefinger over the last three fingers of your right hand. This type of grip is used by a high percentage of Tour professionals.

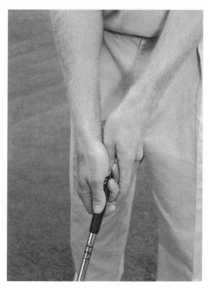

This type of grip, used by many pros, will tame your wrist action.

HOW TO HANDLE BIG
RIGHT–TO–LEFT BREAKERS

Play the ball nearer your right foot to ensure that the putter-face remains, if anything, open and that you keep the ball on the high side of the hole. Also make sure never to let the heel of the putter hit the ball. Last, accelerate the putter through the impact zone.

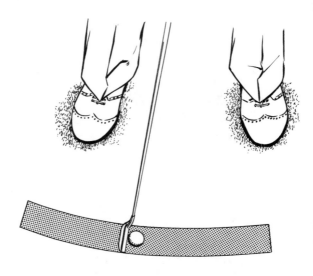

*Play the ball nearer your right foot when
facing a right-to-left putt.*

POINT YOUR THUMBS STRAIGHT DOWN THE SHAFT

Point your thumbs straight down the shaft of the putter to keep the palms of your hands parallel to each other and enhance your feel for the stroke. Many great putters advocate this grip because it also reduces any twisting of the hands during the stroke.

Point both of your thumbs down the shaft to enhance your putting feel.

STAND UP STRAIGHTER
ON LONG PUTTS

When facing a putt of over thirty feet, stand tall with less flex in your knees to enhance your perception of the ball-to-hole line. This address position will also allow your arms to hang naturally under your shoulders and promote a free swing of the putter on the backswing and downswing. Furthermore, the more erect your posture, the better your perception of the target line and hole.

*Stand straighter to promote a freer
swinging action of the putter.*

LEAN YOUR WEIGHT RIGHT

If you seem to be bouncing the ball instead of rolling it smoothly across the green, you're probably putting too much weight on your left foot at address. Remedy your problem by setting up with 60 percent of your weight on your *right* foot. Now putt; you'll see the difference immediately!

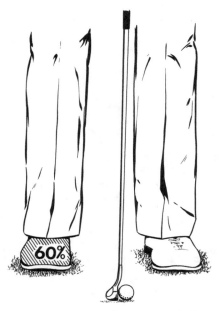

*Putting more weight on your right foot
can sometimes help your stroke.*

SQUARE YOUR BODY TO THE TARGET

To sink more putts from that all-familiar, nerve-racking two-foot range, take a lesson from George Archer and Tom Kite. These two top short-range putters set up with their feet, knees, hips, and shoulders parallel or *square* to the target line. So should you.

A square address position can improve your short-range putting.

HOW TO EMPLOY A NATURAL–RHYTHM STROKE

To promote a smooth inside, down-the-line stroke common to great putters such as Brad Faxon and Ben Crenshaw, align your eyes inside (not over) the ball-to-hole line.

To promote a natural-rhythm stroke, align your eyes inside the target line.

GRIP THE CLUB LIGHTLY

One of the surest ways to enhance your feel for judging distance is to hold the club more lightly than firmly. On a scale of one to ten (one being very light and ten being very firm), use a grip pressure that does not exceed three.

If you're holding the club correctly, a friend should be able to pull the putter out of your hands easily. Also, when you stroke your putts there will be a very slight *play* in the shaft.

On a scale of one to ten, a grip
pressure of three or less is best.

On windy days, it's easy to lose your balance. Therefore, when putting, *widen* your stance by a few inches to build a strong foundation for staying steady over the ball and employing a solid back-and-through stroking action.

*When putting on windy days, widen your
stance to promote a steady stroke.*

LOOK, NO GLOVE!

The majority of professional golfers wear a glove when hitting every shot during a round of golf—except when putting. The reason is that holding the putter in their bare hands enhances their feel, or touch.

Because touch is extra critical on the greens, try taking your glove off when putting. You may be surprised by the difference it makes.

You probably will gain more putting feel by putting without a golf glove.

WHAT TO DO WHEN PUTTING INTO GRAIN

When the blades of grass along the ball-to-hole line are running toward you, there will be a dullness to the green (when running toward the hole, the green will be shiny). In this situation, hit the ball more firmly, making sure to accelerate the putterhead past the ball.

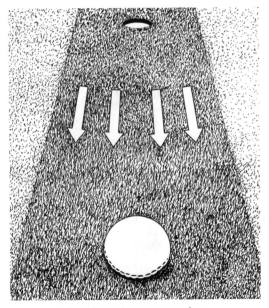

When the grain runs toward you,
hit the ball more firmly than usual.

WHEN DESPERATE,
GO SOUTHPAW STYLE

If you practice hard and just can't get the knack of putting or if you have the yips, try putting left-handed (or right-handed if you normally putt left-handed). This might sound like an off-the-wall tip, but trust me, it can work. The reason is that trying something new will totally alter your mind-set, help you relax, and hole putts, simply because you don't expect to do anything miraculous.

*If you can't get the knack of putting
right-handed, putt southpaw style.*

TRY A PIGEON–TOED STANCE

Moving off the ball, or swaying the body away from the target, is a very common problem among amateur golfers. If you think this might be the reason for your putting problems, try setting up with a pigeon-toed stance, like Arnold Palmer. This unorthodox address position will surely lock you into position and keep you steady throughout the stroke.

*Setting up with a pigeon-toed stance
will prevent you from swaying.*

THE SECRET TO SINKING VERY LONG PUTTS

If you leave putts of fifty or more feet—well short of the hole—and tend to have poor directional control, allow your right wrist to hinge slightly on the backswing. This adjustment will make your stroke less mechanical, enhancing your feel for the correct distance.

Top lag putters have some play in the wrists, so don't freeze them when facing a long putt.

Enhance your feel on long putts by allowing your right wrist to hinge.

TRY THIS PRACTICE DRILL TO HELP YOU JUDGE PACE BETTER

If you're one of those golfers who habitually hits long putts well past the hole, here's a practice drill that will help you learn to pace or *feed* the ball to the hole.

Drop a few balls down on the practice green, about thirty to fifty feet from the fringe on the opposite side. Next, hit a ball across the green and try to have it stop just short of the fringe. Repeat. Keep practicing until none of the balls hits the border between the green and the fringe.

Learn to pace putts by trying to stop the ball short of the fringe grass.

HOW TO MASTER THE SHORT PUTT

If short putts give you trouble, conquer your fears with this drill:

Place three balls three feet away from the hole, three balls four feet away, and three balls five feet away. Stroke a putt into the hole. Repeat. When you're able to sink all nine balls consecutively, you'll feel confident that you've succeeded under pressure.

Remember your success with this drill when you face a short putt on the course.

This "nine-ball" drill will help you become a better short-range putter.

POP YOUR PUTTS

If your normally smooth, arms-and-shoulders pendulum-style putting stroke gets too stiff or starts to promote clubhead deceleration, employ a *pop* stroke by hinging your right wrist on the backstroke and holding that position on the downswing and into impact—all the time limiting the movement of the top end of the putter.

A firm pop stroke will send the ball rolling nicely along the target line.

HOW TO GROOVE A PURE PENDULUM STROKE—FAST

To groove an even-tempo, straight-back and straight-through pendulum stroke, set up with the toe end of the putter pointing at the back of the ball. Next, make a stroke. When you can roll the ball nicely across the green consistently, hold the putter normally and swing. Immediately, you'll realize how easy it now is to make a pure pendulum putting stroke.

Hit putts with the toe of the putter to groove a pure pendulum stroke.

HOW TO ENHANCE
YOUR FEEL

If you're one of those golfers who just has no feel on the greens and is willing to try anything, here's a tip that might work.

When gripping the putter, place your right forefinger straight down the putter's grip, crooking its tip under the shaft (instead of around it).

If your golfing partners tell you that your new grip is ridiculous, tell them former Masters champions Craig Stadler and Seve Ballesteros have used this grip with much success throughout their careers. If that doesn't stop them from needling you, the putts you hole will.

Gripping the club like Stadler and Ballesteros can enhance your touch.

CURE FOR
CHOPPY STROKE

Many club-level golfers lift the putter high off the ground in the backswing. This swing fault causes them to deliver the putter into the ball from too steep an angle.

If you are a quick picker-upper, set the putterblade down at least two inches or more *behind* the ball and start the stroke from there. This unorthodox setup will help you keep the putter low to the ground throughout the stroke and put a purer roll on the ball.

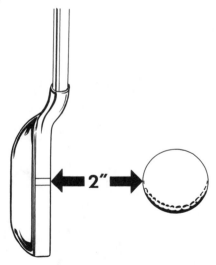

*To cure a chop-action, set the putter
at least two inches behind the ball.*

LOCK IN YOUR ARMS

Players who pull most of their putts during a round usually have a faulty arm or wrist action. When the arms move away from the body on the backstroke, the tendency is for the putter to be pulled across the line coming through.

To remedy this problem and straighten out your putts, rest the butt end of the putter and the back of your left hand against your left thigh, like Billy Casper, who is regarded as one of the all-time greats on the greens.

*This setup, made famous by Billy Casper,
can improve your putting.*

CURE FOR PEEKING

If you look up before the moment of impact and mishit the putt, the following practice drill will help you learn to keep your head still and eyes on the ball until after impact.

Place a ball down about three inches away from the base of a wall. Next, rest the top of your head against the wall, so your eyes are looking down at the ball. Now swing the putter back and through, concentrating on keeping your head dead still and the toe end of the clubhead close to the wall.

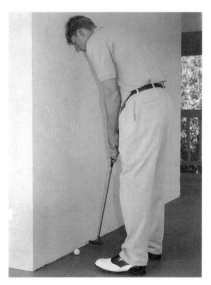

If "peeking" is your problem,
this putting drill will stop it.

To help improve your putting accuracy, lay a chalk line down on the practice green, so it stretches straight out from the front center of one of the holes to a point ten feet away.

Practice for about an hour a week hitting balls from different points along that chalk line and you'll notice how quickly your hole-out conversion rate improves.

Hit putts along a chalk line to improve your putting accuracy.

WATCH THE HOLE
NOT THE BALL

If the direction of a putt is a little off but the pace is good, the ball will come to rest only a couple of inches to the side of the hole. However, if you misjudge the speed, particularly on very fast greens, the ball can come to rest several feet away from the hole.

To help you match the length of a putt to the strength of stroke, practice the following drill:

Assume your normal putting setup and sole the putterhead squarely behind the ball and to the hole. Turn your head and focus your eyes on the hole. Keep your head in that position and make a stroke.

Try this drill from different distances. Soon you'll stop thinking of the stroke and concentrate on the target. You'll also cure your *hit impulse.*

To remedy the "hit impulse" hit putts while looking at the hole.

HOW TO GROOVE A GOOD SHORT STROKE

On longer putts, the putterhead should swing on an inside-square-inside path. However, on short putts you want to swing the putter straight back and straight through along the target line.

To groove this motion, practice putting between two rows of tees.

This drill will help you groove a straight-back, straight-through stroke.

HOW TO MAKE
A RELAXED STROKE

If you're a golfer who holds the putter with a death grip and makes a very slow, very tense stroke, here's a simple tip to help you relax your muscles and employ a smooth putting action.

Raise the putterhead about one-half inch off the green and start your stroke from that position.

Do not form a tripod with the putterhead and your two feet. Try this off-the-ground style or hold the putter lightly on the green.

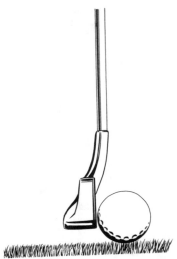

*Hold the putter about a half-inch off
the ground to smoothen your stroke.*

Most great putters use either their left side or right side to control the stroke. So should you.

Being a *one-sided* putter will make you rely less on timing both sides of the body. It will also heighten both your concentration and confidence levels. Don't allow your right side to fight your left side. Make one side completely dominant.

Be a right-sided putter like this player,
or a left-side dominant putter.

HOW TO FIND YOUR PUTTER'S SWEET SPOT

Hitting the ball with the *sweet spot* of the putter's face will allow the ball to roll more smoothly along the ground and hold its line better.

The majority of putters you'll find in your local pro shop feature a dot or some kind of marking, indicating the position of the sweet spot. If you like the look of a putter featuring no sweet spot marking, here's how to find it.

Hold the butt end of the putter handle very lightly with your thumb and forefinger, with the club suspended vertically so that the putterhead's hitting area or *face* is facing you. Next, tap different areas of the face with a coin. When you hit the sweet spot, the putter will swing straight back and then toward you.

*Tapping a coin against the putter's face
will help you find the sweet spot.*

ARE YOU HITTING THE SWEET SPOT?

To check that you're hitting the ball with the sweet spot of the putter, do what Chi Chi Rodriguez does: Dip a ball in a glass of water (or put a little talcum powder on the ball), then putt. Next, look at the face of the putterhead to see where contact was made. If you missed the sweet spot, make the necessary changes in your address position or stroke until you get it right.

Hitting a wet ball can help you detect a putting fault quickly.

WHAT TO DO IF YOUR PUTTS DON'T REACH THE HOLE

If the tempo of your stroke slows on the downswing, you will consistently leave putts short.

To cure this problem, add strips of lead tape to the back of your putter and practice putting for a couple of hours. Take the tape off and putt. You'll feel immediately how much lighter the putter feels and how improved your tempo is.

Practicing with a heavier putter can help you remedy your slow-tempo problem.

ONE WAY TO STOP PULLING PUTTS

If you're pulling putts and you've discovered that a faulty hand position or shoulder alignment is not at fault, the lie of the putter is probably too upright. Ask your pro to give you a flatter-model putter to test and see if it makes a difference.

*The putter featuring a flat lie (left)
can stop you from pulling putts.*

HOW TO SQUARE THE CLUBFACE AT IMPACT

If you consistently leave the face of the putter open or facing right of the target instead of dead square to it at impact, try pushing or piloting the putter toward the hole with the palm of your right hand. Use the same basic technique that you would to roll a ball across a green, using only your right hand.

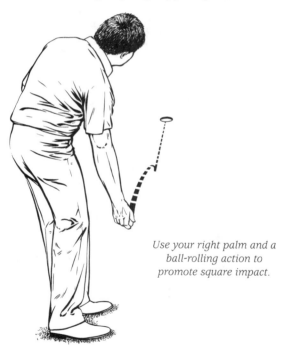

Use your right palm and a ball-rolling action to promote square impact.

HOW TO MAKE A FREER ARM SWING

If you get the sensation that your hands and arms are being blocked by your body when you swing the putter into impact, try standing *open,* with your feet pointing left of the target line. This setup adjustment will allow your arms to swing freely and also improve your view of the line to the hole.

Jackie Burke, who in my opinion is one of the most brilliant people in golf, has always encouraged the open setup alignment.

*An open stance can improve your view
of the hole and stroking action.*

HAVE YOUR CADDY
HOLD THE FLAGSTICK

If glare from the sun or shadows from overhanging branches disrupt your depth perception, have a caddy or one of your playing partners *tend* the flagstick. Even if the putt is short, don't be embarrassed to ask for assistance. Seeing that flagstick in the hole will sharpen your focus.

*Having a caddy hold the flagstick can
enhance your depth-perception.*

HOW TO HELP YOU
LINE UP THE PUTTER

Many golfers have trouble setting the putter down squarely to the hole, particularly if it is over twenty feet away.

If you have this problem, pick out a dark or light spot of grass on the green about three feet in front of you. Roll the ball over that spot and the ball will find the hole.

*Roll the ball over a spot along
the target line and you can't miss!*

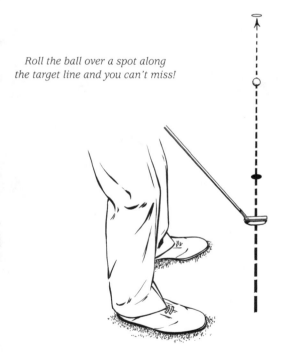

TAKE DEAD AIM

If you want to get the dead-aim feeling when you stand over a putt, set your eyes over the target line but behind the ball, as Jack Nicklaus does.

This setup adjustment will give you a better view of the ball-to-hole line than you would have if you simply set your eyes over the ball.

Setting your eyes over the target line gives you that dead-aim feeling.

CROUCH TO ROLL IN THOSE TEN FOOTERS

If you're not sinking as many putts as you think you should from the ten-foot-and-under range, crouch more at address like Arnold Palmer, Tom Watson, Jack Nicklaus, and other great putters do when they face a short or shortish putt.

*Crouch more over the ball, à la Watson style,
to hole more ten-foot putts.*

SLOW YOUR STROKE
IN THE AFTERNOON

In the afternoon, particularly on very busy public and resort courses, the greens can become considerably faster because of heavy morning play and the wind and sun drying them out. So be sure to hit some practice lag putts before teeing off, and employ a slightly *slower* stroke.

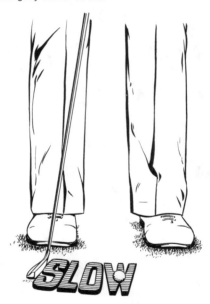

*In the afternoon, when the greens
are faster, employ a slower stroke.*

VARY YOUR SETUP
TO FIX A SLUMP

If the putts just won't drop, start by changing one or more elements of your setup.

You'll be amazed how little things, such as widening your stance, moving the ball up in your stance, or putting slightly more weight on your left foot, can make a difference.

*Changing just one element of your
setup can turn your putting around.*

PRACTICE PROPERLY

Mix up your practice to ready yourself for the variety of putting situations you'll face on the course. Putt one right-to-left putt, then a left-to-right putt, then a straight putt, then a medium length putt, then a short putt, and so on.

Practice hitting more putts in the over-forty-foot range to hone your feel and touch.

*Hitting long putts should always
be part of your practice routine.*

HOW TO MASTER
THE KNEE KNOCKER

If you really want to turn into a putting machine and hole every three-foot putt you face, practice this drill at home:

Each evening before going to bed, hit twenty-five straight putts into a bedpost three feet away.

When you go to the golf course, practice hitting short putts to a tee peg. On each putt, freeze your knees and accelerate the putter toward the target.

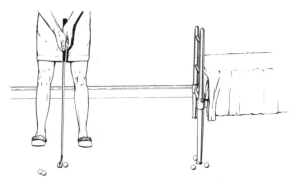

*This "bedpost" drill can help you improve
your short-putt conversion rate.*

THE NUMBER–ONE PRIORITY IN PICKING A PUTTER

Too often golfers are swayed by advertisements that appear in magazines or on television. In choosing a putter, ignore the latest trends and concentrate instead on aesthetics. The putter that looks good and feels solid when you hit putts (no matter how old) is the one that will instill confidence in you and allow you to hole more putts than ever before.

When choosing a new putter,
pay close attention to its "look."

LINE UP YOUR HANDS
WITH THE BALL

Many high-handicap golfers push putts to the right of the hole because they set up with their hands well ahead of the ball.

To make the smoothest possible level stroke and keep the putterface square to the hole, set up with your hands *in line* with the ball.

Set your hands in line with the ball to promote a level putting stroke.

KEEP YOUR HEAD STILL

No two putters have identical strokes. Yet, the very best putters
the game, such as Brad Faxon, all adhere to particular fundamental
one of which is to keep the head *steady* during the stroke, as if
were in a box and unable to move.

*The best putters in the world keep
their heads steady during the stroke.*

In baseball, when a batter is distracted by a negative thought or something else, he or she steps out of the batter's box. Apply the same strategy to golf.

If, when readying yourself to putt, a negative thought pops into your head, step out of the "golfer's box" and start your pre-stroke routine over again.

*If you are distracted when getting ready to
putt, start your routine over.*

STAY FOCUSED

Keep your eyes focused on one spot on the ball during the stroke and after impact, too, as if the ball were still there. Golf's number-one player, Nick Faldo, is one of the best at doing this, simply because he works diligently on "eyeballing" during practice.

The eye movement control centers in your brain are tied into your hand, arm, and shoulder control centers. Moving your eyes during the stroke is a sure ticket to scrambling the "motor program" you had for your stroke.

*Nick Faldo is golf's best player
because his focus on the ball is so good.*

In a recent celebrity golf tournament, basketball star Charles Barkley putted and played very poorly by his own standards.

On the last green, however, he sunk a thirty-foot putt for a birdie. He turned to the crowd and said, "I've been putting like that all day!"

When you do something like that on the last hole, celebrate. Give yourself permission to feel good and forget the not-so-good shots. Feed off the positive results and bring that good attitude to the course the next time you play.

Enjoy great moments on the course—
and remember them for next time.

PRACTICE UNDER STRESSFUL CONDITIONS

I often hear golfers say, "My stroke works great on the practice green, but it doesn't hold up under pressure during regular play." The goal of any good training program, therefore, must be to teach methods that can be performed under pressure.

When practicing, occasionally seek out stressful conditions. Practice when you feel fatigued, when the weather is exceptionally cold, when the greens are especially bad, when you have jet lag, or when there are noisy and potentially distracting conditions. A good practice regimen like this will help you master any putting challenge.

Practicing in cold conditions will make you a stronger competitor.

The more you challenge yourself in practice, the better you will be able to handle pressure when putting on the course. Here are three games that will help you handle the heat.

1. Find the best putter in your club and challenge him or her to an eighteen-hole putting match.

2. Try to make five consecutive short putts with your eyes closed.

3. Putt from thirty-five feet. After the ball comes to rest, penalize yourself by moving it back two feet, so that you never have a tap-in.

Putt against your club's best putter to learn how to handle pressure.

IF YOU MUST ANALYZE, DO IT RIGHT

The typical amateur golfer who misses his or her first practice putt assumes that the bad putt is caused by a faulty setup or stroke. Consequently, he or she starts toying with technique.

Don't judge your putting by one putt. The most effective feedback comes after several putts. Therefore, analyze *blocks* of putts, not just one. That's the only way to make a clear assessment of what's really happening with your putting. Soon there will be very little to fix.

Analyze "blocks" of putts to receive genuine feedback about your putting.

ENVISION A CIRCLE
AROUND THE HOLE

Whenever you face a long putt on very fast greens, don't try to be perfect. Trying to hit perfect putts creates tension and a feeling of being overwhelmed by the challenge. Instead, visualize a circle with a two-foot diameter around the hole and try to lag the ball into that area.

On long putts, lag the ball into an imaginary two-foot area around the hole.

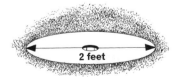

2 feet

PRACTICE PUTTING
AT A DIME

Instead of putting balls toward a hole before a round, make your target a dime set out on the green. Once you're on the course, the 4.25-inch hole will look like a bucket. You'll get that *can't-miss* feeling because you've mastered the harder task of hitting a smaller target.

Practice putting to a dime, and on the course the hole will seem huge.

SLOW DOWN YOUR HEART RATE

If done properly, your preshot putting routine will promote an effortless reduction in heart rate.

Try taking two deep breaths a few seconds before you putt. Research shows that good putters are more in tune with their bodies and can attain a more relaxed, confident approach.

*This player is relaxed at address
because he just took two deep breaths.*

YES, YOU CAN CURE THE YIPS

A *yip* is a nervous jab stroke. If you have the yips, one thing is for certain, you have a bad attitude toward putting, which usually is the result of fear and anxiety. When you're frightened, the body releases adrenaline, affecting blood flow and muscle reaction. Your touch goes out the window.

If you feel yourself tightening up, consciously relax the muscles that have unnecessary excess tension. Remind yourself of your putting fundamentals and *see* the ball go into the hole before you putt. This pre-stroke procedure will help you stay focused and will calm you, too, so your stroke stays smooth.

To employ a smooth stroke like this one, think "fundamentals first."

HOW TO BOOST
YOUR CONFIDENCE

If you're anxious about aligning the club to the ball squarely, place the ball on the green with its trademark pointing on the line you want to start your putt on.

This preswing addition to your putting system will help you set the putter square to the hole and, in turn, boost your level of confidence in your alignment.

*The ball's trademark can help you
align the putter square to your target.*

READ THE GREEN
BEFORE YOU PUTT

In analyzing the slopes in a green, look at the line (or *read* it) from behind the ball, from behind the hole, and from both sides of the ball-to-hole line.

This kind of preparation will alleviate anxiety and thus enable you to make a technically sound, tension-free stroke.

*Looking at the break from the side
of the hole will help you greatly.*

THINK SMART

If you're self-conscious—worried about what your stroke looks like, if you are playing fast enough, if you look like a pro when setting up to the ball—don't be. Instead of seeing yourself from the outside in, focus from the inside out: pay attention to what's outside—the hole. See the ball rolling along the proper line. Become absorbed in your putting—not in yourself.

See the ball rolling nicely off the clubface before you putt.

LET THE BRAIN MAKE THE STROKE FOR YOU

When you throw a baseball to first base, do you think about how far you are from the other player? No, you simply toss the ball, letting your brain calculate and figure out automatically how far the arm must go back and through.

Bring this approach to the putting green. Let your mind focus on the hole instead of the mechanics, and you'll employ a much smoother stroke and hit better putts.

Focusing on the hole will help you "read" the distance of the putt.

If you're an intense golfer who misses putts because you put too much pressure on yourself to hole out, adopt a "de-awfulizing" attitude. Before you start your stroke say to yourself, "If I hole this putt—great; if I don't, it's not the end of the world."

Your new attitude is bound to relax you and thus improve the flow of your putting.

"If I hole this putt great; if I don't, it's not the end of the world."

To help you relax over a putt, realize missing is not the end of the world.

VISUALIZE YOUR FOLLOW–THROUGH FIRST

Leaving putt after putt short? Here's what to do: See yourself following through before you putt. This mental image will encourage you to accelerate the putter nicely through the ball and hit it more affirmatively.

*To promote a solid stroke, see yourself
follow through before you putt.*

TALK YOURSELF OUT OF NEGATIVE THINKING

Top PGA Tour players are able to fight off negative thinking by countering it with positive self-talk. So should you.

When you imagine missing a short putt, stop, take a couple of deep breaths, then say to yourself: "This is fun; I love the challenge of performing under pressure; I *will* hit a good putt."

Before starting the stroke, tell yourself you'll hit a good putt—and you will!

KNOW THYSELF

Justin Leonard won the 1993 United States Amateur Championship, the 1994 NCAA Championship, and numerous collegiate and regional amateur events in 1993.

What caused this sudden domination of amateur golf? Justin made a significant change in his mental strategy that opened the door to lower scores. He and his coach, Randy Smith, determined that, based on his ball striking and short-game mastery as well as his mental toughness, he was playing and putting too conservatively. Justin made a thoughtful decision to be more "mentally aggressive" in his attack of the hole. Lower scores followed.

Assess the state of your short game and putting—if your skills are high, be aggressive. If you haven't mastered the skills, be more patient and conservative.

Thinking of banging the ball in the back of the cup is a good strategy.

HOW TO INTENSIFY YOUR CONCENTRATION

During practice, hit putts using the leading edge of a wedge. You will have to concentrate extra hard and make good eye-to-ball focus if you want the club to meet the equator of the ball, rolling it smoothly as a putter would.

*Putting with a wedge will train
you to concentrate more intensely.*

HOW TO GET IN THE ZONE

A quiet mind is essential to good putting. One sure and simple way to tune out and get into the *isolation chamber* is to pull down your golf cap, so its brim is just above your eyes. You'll be locked in and better able to block out distractions.

*Pull down the brim of your hat
to tune out any distractions.*

If your putting distance and direction control are inconsistent, you're probably exaggerating the hinging action of your wrists during the backswing. To encourage a dead-wristed, arms-and-shoulders pendulum-style stroke, imagine that your hands and wrists are cast in concrete.

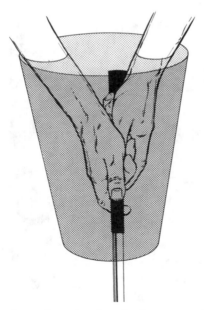

Pretend your hands and wrists are cast in concrete to promote a solid stroke.

DON'T TAKE GIMMES

If you're like most amateur golfers, you welcome a playing partner telling you your short putt is good, meaning, of course, that the shot has been conceded.

If play is slow, by all means take the gimme. However, if the pace of play is moving along nicely, putt very short putts. The reason is that if you putt the ball in a casual match, you'll build up the confidence that you need to hole the putt in a serious match.

*You'll gain in the long run
if you putt "gimme" putts.*

PLAY WITH YOUR PRACTICE MIND-SET

Putting practice performed with a good attitude (feeling challenged, enthusiastic, and positive about what you are doing) will enhance your performance.

The key is to keep this attitude when you get to the course. If you were having fun and were relaxed during practice, bring this same attitude to the course.

If you change your attitude in competition to a more negative, anxious, fearful approach, you're likely to alter the motor memory of your putting stroke.

Take your relaxed practice attitude to the golf course.

WHAT TO DO WHEN
PUTTING DOWNHILL

When you face a severe downhill putt on a slick green, imagine that the hole is closer to you. This mental image will help you make a more confident putting stroke. More important, because you have altered your goal, you will not hit the ball well past the hole.

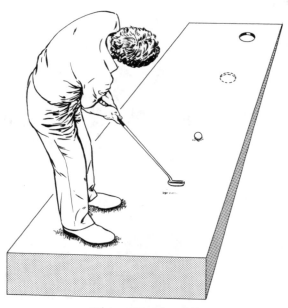

*When putting downhill,
imagine the hole is closer to you.*

On the day of a big match, practice putting with only one ball. This strategy will allow you to simulate the one-trial, one-ball *game situation,* and force you to put on your best game face. There are no mulligan putts on the course.

*Practice putting with one ball
to simulate the course situation.*

HOW TO HELP YOUR TEACHER HELP YOU

If you're working on a putting improvement program with your teacher, it will help if you keep a journal that details your putting performance during a round. Record your notes while the round is still fresh in your mind. That way, when you see your instructor for a lesson, he or she can help you help yourself. Your teacher will help you analyze trends and tendencies, such as too many three-putts when you have makable short birdie putts.

Recording your putting performances in a journal will help your teacher help you.

WHAT TO DO WHEN PUTTING UPHILL

When you face a severe uphill putt, imagine that the hole is a few feet farther away. This mental image will help you make a more aggressive stroke and ensure that you reach the hole.

*When putting uphill, pretend
the hole is a few feet farther away.*

HOW TO BRING YOUR
NEW STROKE INTO BATTLE

The hardest thing about dealing with the yips is not regrooving a good stroke. Rather it is taking your new stroke to the golf course that first time and wondering whether you will yip or not. You will until you can prove to yourself that you can putt to your old good standard.

To help encourage this good stroke, make your practice stroke a purposeful rehearsal of the successful one to come.

*Make your practice stroke a rehearsal
of the good stroke to come.*

FACE THE FACTS

Sometimes you are not to blame for a missed putt. The fact is, imperfections in the green, such as spike marks, can keep a perfectly stroked putt out of the hole. So don't be too quick to get down on yourself or to change your stroke.

*When you miss, realize a spike mark—
not a bad stroke—could be at fault.*

MAKE THE PUTT IN YOUR HEAD FIRST

The great Jack Nicklaus once said that he never missed a putt in his mind before he actually started his stroke. Learn from Jack's wisdom. When you are standing over a putt readying yourself to start the stroke, imagine the ball rolling along a line to the hole and dropping in the cup. Seeing the putt drop will give you the mental edge you need to hole out under pressure.

Take a lesson from Jack Nicklaus:
see the ball "drop" before you putt.

As important as the stroke is, it's not everything. If you start thinking too much about technique, you'll start ignoring conditions that might affect the roll of the ball, such as a strong wind or wet greens.

A good preround practice policy is to assess the conditions. If, for example, you learn that the greens are windblown and extra fast, you'll be able to putt with less self-doubt and more confidence.

When practicing, assess the green's condition so that you're ready for play.

HOW TO PSYCH
YOURSELF DOWN

When you are putting in a big match or championship, it's more important to be able to psych *down* than psych *up*.

One great way to calm down is to clean out any negative thoughts from your mind's attic. Rather than setting up to putt and thinking, "If I miss this putt, I'll be so far behind my opponent, I'll never catch up," keep your head clear. Only positive thoughts, such as "I'll hole this," should be allowed to enter your awareness.

*When standing over a tough pressure
putt like this one, think positive.*

HIT THE CAN AND
YOU'LL SINK MORE PUTTS

Hit putts to a beverage can set out on the green. After about a dozen putts, stick the can in the cup. You'll see that the can's circumference is considerably smaller than the cup's.

Now, the real secret to success: on the course, visualize the can above the cup and even with the ground. Seeing the can will make you less hole conscious and encourage a good stroke.

*Imagery such as this will encourage
a confident putting stroke.*

STAY COOL

To maximize your performance on the course, never get overexcited after making a putt or distressed after missing a putt. Stay focused and concentrate on the shot in front of you—not the last putt you made or missed.

With this kind of Fred Couples–style attitude, you'll stay mentally sharp and physically relaxed. You won't have to force good scores; they'll just happen.

When you miss a putt,
it's important to stay cool.

COMMITMENT IS COMMITMENT IS COMMITMENT

Real commitment means *zero self-doubt*. So if your coach recommends trying something new, such as a reverse overlap putting grip, believe in it with all your heart.

If your coach recommends a new grip like this one, believe in it.

DURING THE IMPROVEMENT STAGE, DON'T BE AFRAID TO FAIL

If you're working out problems that require you to alter your setup and stroke, you must expect that things might get worse before they get better. What's *overlearned* and normal for you will have a tendency to affect (negatively) what you're trying to do. However, don't revert to your old stroke. Hang in there and stay patient while you correct your mechanics. Before you know it, everything will come together and you'll forget your stroke was ever *sick*.

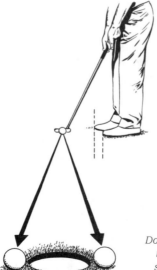

Don't be afraid to fail when trying a new setup key, such as an open stance.

ONE MENTAL KEY IS PLENTY

Thinking too much about the complexities of the stroke can disrupt its flow. So bring only one mental key to the course, such as hitting the middle of the ball with the middle of the putterface.

*Try to hit the middle of the ball
with the middle of the putterface.*

CLOSE YOUR EYES TO LEARN DISTANCE CONTROL

New golfers, particularly, have no clue about matching a distance to a length of stroke. To learn this skill quickly, hit putts with your eyes closed and guess how far you hit the ball before looking up. After just a few practice sessions, you'll have a complete database in your brain and thus be able to just look at the hole and know exactly how long a stroke to make.

*Putt with your eyes closed
to enhance your feel for distance.*

PLAY MIND GAMES TO HELP YOU PUTT BETTER

If you consistently hit the ball so far past the hole that you set yourself up for a three-putt, this practice tip will help you improve your distance control:

As you line up a putt, imagine a steep cliff about two feet behind the hole. This mental image will train you to lag the ball nicely up to the hole, and if you do hit the ball past the hole, it will be within easy tap-in range.

This mental image will prevent you from hitting the ball far past the hole.

RECALL YOUR EASY PRACTICE–GREEN STROKE

The next time you get nervous while preparing to hit a pressure putt, calm yourself down by imagining yourself holing these on the practice green. This image will make you more relaxed so that you will make a pressure-proof putting stroke and knock the ball straight into the cup.

When preparing to hit a must-make putt, imagine holing out in practice.

STICK TO YOUR GAME PLAN

Evander Holyfield lost his first fight with Riddick Bowe because he failed to stick to his game plan. He won the rematch because he stuck to a set game plan.

Don't ever get away from your game plan on the golf course, i.e., do not make an irrational decision to charge a putt in what is not a must-make situation. Stick to a rational game plan based on knowing what you *can* do.

On putts like this, stick to your game plan and lag the ball.

PRETEND YOUR SHOULDERS ARE A SEESAW

Here's a tip on how to employ a pure pendulum stroke. It was given to me by my friend Joey Sindelar, Jr., a fine player on the PGA Tour.

Joey's father taught him to pretend that his shoulders work like a seesaw. On the backstroke, lower your left shoulder so that your right shoulder rocks upward and the putterface swings straight back along the ball-to-hole line. On the down-stroke, lower your right shoulder so that your left shoulder rocks upward and the club swings back square to the hole.

Thinking of your shoulders as a seesaw will promote a good stroke.

GO WITH YOUR STRENGTHS

Al Del Greco, of the Houston Oilers football team, is one of the best field-goal kickers in the game. He was also cited as the best golfer among other professional athletes by *Golf* magazine.

Al frequently uses golf images to relax himself before he kicks a field goal, saying to himself for example, "This is just a tap in." On the golf course he has won numerous tournaments, including the 1993 and 1994 NFL Cadillac Senior Tour Challenges. One of his images on the putting green is, "This is just an extra point—just hit it solid."

The next time you feel nervous over a shot, such as a putt off the fringe that you have to hole to stay in the match, trick your brain. Relating to your strengths and what you're familiar with will relax you in a tense on-course situation.

Play mind games with yourself to help you sink putts like this.

SEE A GOLFER PUTTING AT YOU TO READ THE LINE

If you have great difficulty reading the line of a putt, imagine a good golfer hitting toward you from just in front of the hole. See how the ball breaks and then use that read to guide your ball into the hole. Just remember, if the ball breaks right to left when it comes at you, it will break the opposite way when you putt in the opposite direction. Apply the same strategy if the putt breaks from left to right. Straight putts are always straight.

Imagining a player putting toward you can help you read the green's break.

GO WITH THE FLOW

If putts on speedy greens cause you problems, try this mental tip:

Imagine a rapid stream of water flowing from the ball toward the hole. This image will encourage you to stroke the ball lightly, so that it starts rolling along the correct line, then rolls to the hole at the proper speed.

*On very fast greens,
just "go with the flow."*

HAVE FUN

When standing over a putt to win a big match, say to yourself, "This is fun." Just that one line will help you relax and enjoy the challenge of competition.

When standing over a putt to win a match, tell yourself, "This is fun."

TRY THIS
CONCENTRATION TRIGGER

If you're one of those golfers who gets mentally lazy on the greens, make it your business to start concentrating more intensely the second you pull the Velcro strap open on your glove and take it off to putt.

*Pulling on the Velcro of your glove is
your signal to concentrate intently.*

HIT THE IMAGINARY BALL ON BREAKING PUTTS

On undulating greens featuring big breaks, aim to hit an imaginary ball set out on the green where you figure the putt will start to break. If you hit the imaginary ball with the proper pace, you've made the putt you intended to make!

Hit an imaginary ball to help you sink more breaking putts.

TRUST YOUR STROKE

Greg Norman won the 1993 British Open at Royal St. George's Golf Club, in the UK, with a phenomenal final round of 64.

One reason he scored so well was great putting. What made him stroke so smoothly through the ball and hole putts was one final thought he had before he swung the putter back: "Trust yourself, trust your stroke."

The same positive thought process will help you putt better too.

Trust your stroke to hit smoothly through the ball, like Greg Norman does.

A HEALTHY MIND COMES FROM A HEALTHY BODY

Stimulants such as caffeine (found in coffee, tea and soft drinks) can make you physically jumpy and mentally unfocused. This is obviously not the state of mind you want to be in when you're facing a pressure putt to win a big match.

Proper hydration before you play is always important but especially before a match. So before competing, replace the "social drugs" with a high protein drink or a bottle of mineral water. You'll find yourself feeling mentally sharper and physically better able to make a smooth putting stroke.

Drinking mineral water before a round of golf is a healthy policy.

ABOUT THE AUTHORS

JIM McLEAN is the golf director at the Doral Resort and Country Club in Miami, Florida. Known best for his reputation as a teacher, McLean instructs many of the top PGA Tour pros, including 1992 U.S. Open winner Tom Kite and 1993 Australian Open champion Brad Faxon.

McLean, who is a teaching editor for *Golf* magazine, has authored both *The Golf Digest Book of Drills* and *The Eight-Step Swing* and also produced the highly successful video *Ten Fundamentals of the Modern Golf Swing*.

A fine player, too, McLean won the 1989 National Skins Team Championship with amateur partner George Zahringer.

FRAN PIROZZOLO is chief of the Neuropsychology Service at the Baylor College of Medicine in Houston, Texas. He was a member of the prestigious National Academy of Sciences Committee on Techniques to Enhance Human Performance. He is also a consultant to several golf-learning centers, golf-equipment companies, and NASA.

Pirozzolo has written many articles for leading sports magazines, including *Golf* magazine, and has authored eleven books on the brain and behavior.

Pirozzolo works on performance enhancement with many of the world's best golfers, the Houston Astros baseball team, members of the Houston Oilers football team and of U.S. Olympic teams, and other athletes from the world of boxing, basketball, tennis, and shooting sports.

KEN LEWIS is recognized as one of the world's leading golf illustrators.

JEFF BLANTON is a renowned Florida-based golf photographer whose work has appeared in several books and magazines.